BROKEN ROSE

A COLLECTION OF
MELANCHOLY MUSINGS

SHOAIB MOHAMMAD

Made with ♥ on the Notion Press Platform
www.notionpress.com

Dedicated to:

You & life,

for providing me with endless experiences and emotions to put into words.

Thank you for being a part of my journey.

With love and gratitude,

Shoaib Mohammad

Contents

Contents

Foreword

Dear readers,

It is with great pleasure that I present to you this collection of poems. Within these pages, you will find a tapestry of emotions, experiences, and perspectives woven together to create a unique and powerful narrative.

As you journey through the poems in this book, you will encounter themes of love, loss, hope, and perseverance, as well as a celebration of the beauty of the world around us. Each poem is a reflection of my own personal experiences, as well as the experiences of those around me. They are a testament to the resilience of the human spirit and the enduring power of the written word.

I hope that these poems will speak to you in a meaningful way, and that they will touch your heart and stir your soul. Whether you are seeking solace, inspiration, or simply a moment of quiet contemplation, I believe that you will find it within these pages.

So, take a moment to breathe, to relax, and to immerse yourself in the words on these pages. I hope that you will find, as I have, that poetry has the power to heal, to comfort, and to inspire.

With gratitude,

Shoaib Mohammad

Prologue

In the depths of my mind, lies a world of imagination,

A place where emotions run wild, with a captivating narration.

A land of beauty and grace, where words dance on the page,

A canvas painted with rhyme, that captures life's essence in a cage.

This book is a collection of my thoughts, a journey of self-discovery,

An exploration of the soul, where I share my heart's every story.

It speaks of love and loss, of hope and despair,

Of laughter and tears, and the moments beyond repair.

So open these pages, and enter my mind,

And allow my words to paint pictures, so elegant and divine.

For within these lines, lies a world waiting to be explored,

A kingdom of poetry, where the heart and soul can soar.

1. BROKEN ROSE

Broken Rose,
a symbol of pain
In a garden of flowers,
you remain
With petals as dark as night
You stand out, a stunning sight
Your thorns, a warning so dire
But still,
beauty you inspire
In the hearts of those who see
The grace that lies within thee
Though often seen as ominous
Your grace is truly magnificent
For in the darkness you shine bright
A symbol of beauty
in the night
So here's to you,
dear broken Rose
May you continue to grow and pose
A reminder that in life so true
Beauty can be found in darkness too.
A broken rose, once beautiful and bright,
Now lay in ruins, abandoned in its plight.

Its petals torn, its stem bent and bent,
Its once-strong frame now fragile, spent.
But still it shines, with a gentle grace,
A symbol of hope, in this desolate place.
For though its beauty may be marred by pain,
It still holds within, a love that remains.
For in its brokenness, it tells a tale,
Of a love that lived, and a heart that did prevail.
Of a rose that bloomed, in a garden so fair,
And withstood the storms, with a courage so rare.
So let us hold fast, to the broken rose,
And cherish its beauty, wherever it goes.
For though it may be bent, and its petals torn,
It still holds within, a love that was born.

2. DARKNESS

Darkness,
oh darkness,
a shroud so deep,
A veil that covers, a world to keep.
The light is gone,
the stars are dim,
Yet in this void, a peace begins.
a cloak that covers the land
A veil that shrouds with a gentle hand
A mystery that makes the heart race
A silence that fills with a sense of grace
In the night, it brings serenity
A peaceful calm that sets us free
From the chaos of a busy day
It gives us time to pause
and pray
Darkness,
oh darkness,
a shroud so deep,
A veil that covers, a world to keep.
The light is gone,
the stars are dim,
Yet in this void, a peace begins.

It wraps around, a comforting hold,

A stillness found,

a story untold.

The night is quiet, the moon aglow,

Its silver light,

a gentle show.

The shadows dance,

a graceful swirl,

A symphony of darkness and twirl.

The darkness whispers, a gentle muse,

Its secrets kept, a mystery to choose.

So let us embrace, this dark embrace,

And find within, a beauty and grace.

For in the night, we find our peace,

And darkness,

oh darkness,

a gift to keep.

3. WHISPERS

The wind blows soft and low,

Carrying secrets to and fro.

Whispers in the sand they say,

A story waiting to be played.

The grains they dance,

they sing,

they flow,

A symphony, a soothing show.

Of secrets told, of tales untold,

Of memories that never grow old.

The ocean roars, the waves crash high,

But still the whispers do not die.

For they are carried by the wind,

To be heard and seen again.

So listen close,

and you shall hear,

The whispers in the sand, so clear.

A story waiting to be told,

Of love and loss,

of young and old.

Whispers in the Sand

The wind blows soft and low,

Carrying secrets to and fro.

Whispers in the sand they say,
A story waiting to be played.
The grains they dance, they sing, they flow,
A symphony, a soothing show.
Of secrets told, of tales untold,
Of memories that never grow old.
The ocean roars, the waves crash high,
But still the whispers do not die.
For they are carried by the wind,
To be heard and seen again.

4. DARK

a storm that brews within,
A shadow that grows, a weight to bear.
It clouds the mind, a constant din,
And drags the soul, down to despair.
It steals the joy, the light of day,
And leaves behind, a heavy heart.
It's hard to cope, to find a way,
When all that's left, is pain and dark.
But in the storm, a glimmer shines,
A light that beckons, hope to find.
A chance to rise, above the fray,
And break the chains, of depression's hold.
So reach out, don't be afraid to ask,
For help from friends, or a listening ear.
And know that you, are valued and loved,
And together, this storm you can weather.

5. ASHES

Ashes,
oh ashes,
a reminder of flame,
The remnants of fire, a story untold.
Once bright and blazing, now just the same,
A memory of passion, now grey and cold.
The fire that burned, with heat and light,
The life that was lived, now gone in sight.
The passion that flourished, now just a trace,
The love that was shared, now just a space.
But in the ashes, a promise remains,
A spark of new life, that calls our names.
A chance to rise, from the dust and grey,
And create a new tomorrow, with brighter day.
So let us cherish, the memories of fire,
And hold on tight, to the hope that aspires.
For in the ashes, a seed will grow,
And blossom into beauty, for all to know.

6. BLACK PAIN

Black pain,
a burden too heavy to bear,
A weight that drags, a sorrow beyond compare.
It's rooted deep, in the history of time,
A legacy of pain, a constant chime.
The wounds of the past, now a part of today,
The scars of slavery, now a price to pay.
The injustices done, now a constant ache,
The battles won, now a constant stake.
But in the pain, a strength is born,
A resilience forged, a spirit reborn.
For from the ashes, a phoenix will rise,
And with courage and grace, reach for the skies.
So let us stand, with those who suffer,
And fight for a world, where pain is no buffer.
For in their pain, our own is exposed,
And in their struggle, a future is disclosed.

7. SAND

My Sand
dear tale of time,
A journey untold, from shore to shore.
It starts as grains, with dreams so fine,
And travels far, forever more.
The winds of change, they shape its form,
The waves of life,
they ebb
and flow.
And with each step, a tale is born,
A story of grit,
and endless glow.
The deserts sing, a song of heat,
The beaches dance, with waves so bright.
The dunes they rise,
with grace so fleet,
A symphony, of beauty and light.
But in the end,
all stories must end,
And this tale of sand,
must come to close.
Yet in its wake, a legacy extend,
A story of life,

and how it grows.
So let us cherish, oh my sand,
And all that it teaches,
and all that it's planned.
For in its journey,
a lesson we learn,
That time may pass, but
the story will burn.

8. BURDEN

The tree stands tall,
amidst the storm,
Its roots dug deep,
its branches so strong.
It bends and it sways,
with grace and form,
A symbol of life, in nature so long.
The winds they howl, and the rain pours down,
But the tree stands firm, its hold never lost.
It weathers the tempest, with grace so renowned,
A fortress of hope, at any cost.
For the tree has seen, seasons come and go,
And knows the secrets, that only time can hold.
It has learned to bend, and not to break,
And found a resilience, that never grows old.
So let us be like the tree, in the storm,
With roots that dig deep, and branches that soar.
For in the face of life's challenges born,
We too can weather, the winds and the roar.

9. SEA

The deep sea,
a world of mystery,
A realm of darkness, a place so deep.
Where creatures roam, with grace and glee,
And secrets untold, in the depths they keep.
The pressure is high, the light so low,
The shadows so deep, the silence so still.
Yet life thrives here, with a glow so slow,
A beauty untold, on the ocean floor thrill.
The creatures of night, they dance in the dark,
With fins and tentacles, and scales so bright.
They bask in the light, of the bioluminescent spark,
A symphony of life, in the sea's enchanting light.
So let us journey, to the deep below,
And explore this world, of beauty untold.
For in the deep sea, we can find our way,
And bask in the wonder, of life every day.

10. SADNESS

Sadness
creeps upon my soul
Bringing darkness to control
It weighs me down like heavy stone
Leaves me feeling all alone
Memories of joy now fade away
Replaced by tears that never stray
A heart once bright now filled with pain
In this endless cycle, I remain
I try to search for light within
But the clouds of sadness always win
Hope seems so distant, out of reach
As I struggle just to breathe
But still I hold on, day by day
Hoping that the clouds will fade away
For even in the depths of night
A glimmer of hope shines oh so bright
So I'll keep walking, step by step
Hoping to escape this endless depth
For I know that someday I'll see
The happiness that's meant for me.
Hopelessness, a cruel affliction
That grips my heart with icy hand

It steals my strength and steals my light
And leaves me feeling lost and stranded
The world around me seems so bleak
As darkness threatens to consume
It drains my soul and drains my hope
And leaves me feeling all alone
I search for comfort, but in vain
For solace seems so far away

11. HPELESSNESS

The weight of hopelessness is strong
And pulls me down with every day
But still I hold on to a flame
Of courage, burning bright within
For in the depths of deepest night
A glimmer of hope still shines within
I know that life is never easy
And sometimes we must face our fears
But I will keep on fighting on
And hope will guide me through the tears.

12. MEMORIES

A love once bright, now dim and pale
A bond that shattered, unable to withstand the trial
Memories linger, but joy is gone
Heartache echoes, as we both move on
We danced in the sun, laughed in the rain
But now all that's left is hurt and pain
Words left unspoken, love left to die
A once beautiful rose, now wilted and dry
Tears fall like rain, washing away the past
Wishing for a love that could forever last
But some things are not meant to be
And so, my bad love, we not set each other free
The road ahead may be long and rough
But I know I must be strong enough
To mend my broken heart, to he
all and grow
And find a love that's meant to forever glow.

13. UNSPOKEN

A love once shared, now lost in time
A bond that weakened, unable to climb
Fading memories, a heart that aches
Separation brings sorrow that it makes
The laughter has faded, the joy has gone
Leaving emptiness where it once begun
Words left unspoken, love left untold
A relationship that has grown so cold
The road ahead may be uncertain, but I'll find my way
Though the journey ahead may be long and grey
I'll pick up the pieces, of my shattered heart
And start a new journey, a fresh new start
Though the pain may linger, and the tears may flow
I'll find the strength to let love go
For though this separation may cause me pain
It's a necessary step, to start over again.

14. TRUST

Open arms, a warm embrace
A symbol of love, a sacred space
Where two hearts meet, and come alive
In a love that's pure, and truly thrives
Open arms, a sign of trust
A bond that's unbreakable, a love that's just
Where fears subside, and fears take flight
In a love that's fearless, and shines so bright
Open arms, a place of peace
Where two souls unite, in a love that never cease
Where worries fade, and joy takes hold
In a love that's strong, and stories untold
Open arms, a promise of forever
A love that endures, through stormy weather
For in these arms, I'll always be
In a love that's pure, and meant to be.

15. AGAIN

A heart once broken, now mended with care

A soul once lost, now found its repair

Love has returned, with a brighter gleam

Bringing happiness, like a flowing stream

Eyes that once saw, only pain and sorrow

Now gaze upon, a love that they borrow

A smile that once faded, now shines so bright

A love that once ended, now sees new light

With open arms, I welcome this love

For it's a gift from above

A second chance, to feel alive

A chance to fall in love, once more and thrive

Each day a new journey, with love by my side

Each night a peaceful slumber, with joy deep inside

For this love is different, a love that will last

A love that brings happiness, forever surpassing the past.

16. FAILURE

A soul that's weary, a heart that's tired
A mind that's restless, with worries not expired
A journey so long, with battles to fight
A path that's uncertain, with darkness in sight
The road ahead is rough, the journey is tough
With challenges waiting, and mountains to rough
Yet this weary soul, keeps pushing on
With resilience and courage, and a will so strong
For this struggling heart, knows no defeat
It rises again, every time it's beat
With each setback, it becomes more wise
With each failure, it learns to arise
For the journey of life, is not meant to be easy
But it's through the struggles, that our souls become breezy
So let us embrace, the challenges we face
For it's through them, that we find grace.

17. SHADOW

A man once strong, now stands defeated
His spirit broken, his heart deleted
Once a conqueror, now a shadow of the past
His future uncertain, his present aghast
His eyes once bright, now dull with pain
His once confident walk, now filled with strain
Defeat has consumed him, and love has fled
Leaving him alone, in a world full of dread
He looks to the sky, and wonders why
Why life has dealt him this cruel blow
Why he's been abandoned, and left in the snow
His dreams shattered, his spirit low
But in the depths of despair, a spark still glows
A flame that still burns, and never fades
A hope that he'll rise, and take back his throne
And once again, conquer the world with his bravery and stone
So let us not judge this defeated man
For he's just a warrior, in search of his stand
He'll rise again, and reclaim his throne
For his spirit is strong, and his heart is made of stone.

18. WAITING

A heart that's lonely, a soul that's waiting
For a love that's true, a love worth relishing
He stands by the window, and looks at the sky
Hoping and praying, that love will soon arrive
He waits with patience, with an open heart
For a love that's pure, and a work of art
He knows not when, or where it will be
But he waits with hope, for his love to see
His eyes are fixed, on the horizon so far
Hoping for a glimpse, of his guiding star
His heart is filled, with an endless desire
For a love that's real, and never a liar
For love is a treasure, more precious than gold
It's the reason we live, and the reason we grow old
And this waiting heart, will not give up the fight
For love is worth waiting for, and always shining bright.

19. HOPE

Hope is a flame, burning bright and bold
Guiding us through, the darkest nights and cold
It lifts us up, when all seems lost
And gives us strength, at whatever the cost
Hope is a spark, igniting our dreams
Filling our hearts, with joy and beams
It opens our eyes, to endless possibilities
And shows us a world, beyond realities
Hope is a voice, whispering in our ear
Telling us to trust, and never to fear
For with hope we can conquer, every mountain high
And with hope we can soar, towards the clear blue sky
Hope is a promise, that we hold inside
A light that shines, in the darkest of tides
It gives us courage, when all else fails
And with hope, our spirit never pales
So hold on tight, to that spark of hope
For it will lead you, down a path with scope
And always remember, in every trying hour
That hope is the one thing, that will give you power.

20. PROMISE

A promise to love, is a vow so true
A bond between two, forever in view
It's a declaration, of love so rare
A commitment to cherish, and always be there
A promise to love, is a ray of hope
A light in the darkness, a way to cope
It's a warm embrace, in a world so cold
A love that's unbreakable, and worth more than gold
A promise to love, is a bond of trust
A support in life, a love that must
It's a hand to hold, in the darkest night
A love that shines bright, and always feels right
A promise to love, is a path so clear
A journey together, year after year
It's a love that grows, and never fades
A love that endures, through life's many shades
So let us make this promise, and hold it dear
To love with all our heart, and always be near
For love is a gift, that we must nurture and tend
And this promise to love, will forever be our best friend.

21. BOUNDARIES

Love has its boundaries, like the sky so wide
Lines that define it, like the river's tide
It's a space for giving, and receiving too
A safe place for hearts, to grow and be true
Love has its limits, that keep us in check
Guiding our actions, and our words we speak
It's a way of loving, that keeps us from harm
And helps us respect, each other's charm
Love knows its boundaries, and stays within reach
It never crosses, the lines we each teach
It honors our needs, and gives us room to grow
And lets us be who we are, and lets our love show
Love is not blind, it has eyes that can see
It knows what's right, and what's good for thee
It never takes more, than what we can give
And always leaves room, for the soul to live
So let us cherish, the boundaries of love
And respect them always, from heaven above
For they keep us safe, and help us to grow
And allow our love, to continue to flow.

22. DREAM

Together apart, but never alone
Two hearts beating, as one unknown
Waiting for the day, when they'll unite
And bask in love's warm and tender light
Memories and dreams, are all they have
Of each other's laughter, and each other's glad
They write letters, and make plans so grand
Hoping time will pass, and they'll be hand in hand
Every moment, feels like an eternity
But they hold on to hope, and their love's ability
To bring them together, in sweet embrace
And fill their lives, with love and grace
The waiting is hard, but their love is strong
It gives them the courage, to carry on
For they know the end, is just the start
And their love will shine, like a brilliant star
So they wait and they hope, with open arms
For the day they'll meet, and be free from all harm
And their love will flourish, like a blooming rose
In each other's embrace, they'll forever doze.

23. STRESS

Exhausted from life, I long for a rest,
The daily grind has left me depressed.
Days filled with work, nights filled with stress,
I need a break from this constant mess.
I search for solace, I search for peace,
Away from the chaos, a life of ease.
Where I can breathe, where I can be,
And leave behind all my anxiety.
But life is a journey, with twists and turns,
With highs and lows, and lessons to learn.
So I must go on, I must stand tall,
And face my fears, and conquer them all.
For though I am tired, and worn at the core,
I know I will find strength to endure.
With hope in my heart, and a song in my soul,
I'll rise from the ashes, and make me whole.
So I'll take a deep breath, and start anew,
With a smile on my face, and a spirit that's true.
For life is a gift, and I will not waste,
This precious moment, in this precious place.

24. ALONE

In a world full of noise, I stand alone
With memories that haunt me, like an echo unknown
A love that once bloomed, now long gone
Leaving me with a heart, that beats all alone.
I walk the streets, in search of a sign
Of a love that is pure, and truly divine
But all I find is emptiness and a cry
Of a lonely lover, that wants to fly.
The stars up above, shine so bright
But they are distant, and out of sight
And the moon, it whispers a sweet lullaby
But it can't soothe, a lonely lover's sigh.
I close my eyes, and dream of you
Of a love, that was pure and true
But when I open them, I am alone
In this world, where I stand on my own.
But still, I hold on to the hope
That someday, I'll find a way to cope
And my heart, will beat in perfect rhyme
With the love, of a lifetime.

25. SADNESS

In a world of pain, I find myself
With a heart that aches, and a soul in distress
A love that once bloomed, now wilted and dead
Leaving me with memories, I cannot forget.
The skies once bright, now dark with rain
A reflection of the tears, I cannot restrain
The wind whispers a song, so full of sorrow
Of a love that was real, but gone tomorrow.
I wander the streets, lost in my mind
Thinking of the moments, that I left behind
Of laughter and joy, and a love so true
But now all I have, is a heart that's blue.
The night creeps in, and I am alone
With nothing but memories, of what once was known
But I hold on to hope, in the depths of my soul
That someday, my heart will heal, and be whole.
So I'll dance in the rain, and let my tears fall
For the love that I lost, and the sorrow that calls
And when the storm passes, I'll rise up again
With a heart that is strong, and a love that remains.

26. RAIN

In a world of pain, I find myself
With a heart that aches, and a soul in distress
A love that once bloomed, now wilted and dead
Leaving me with memories, I cannot forget.
The skies once bright, now dark with rain
A reflection of the tears, I cannot restrain
The wind whispers a song, so full of sorrow
Of a love that was real, but gone tomorrow.
I wander the streets, lost in my mind
Thinking of the moments, that I left behind
Of laughter and joy, and a love so true
But now all I have, is a heart that's blue.
The night creeps in, and I am alone
With nothing but memories, of what once was known
But I hold on to hope, in the depths of my soul
That someday, my heart will heal, and be whole.
So I'll dance in the rain, and let my tears fall
For the love that I lost, and the sorrow that calls
And when the storm passes, I'll rise up again
With a heart that is strong, and a love that remains.

27. WAITING

In the midst of the night, I wander alone
In search of a love, that has yet to be shown
With a heart that beats, and a soul that yearns
For a love that is real, and a fire that burns.
I walk the streets, with a longing so deep
For a love that's pure, and one I can keep
And I listen for whispers, on the wind so light
Of a love that's waiting, just out of sight.
The stars up above, they twinkle and shine
A reflection of the hope, that I have in mind
And the moon, it shines a silver light
Guiding me forward, on my quest tonight.
I'll keep searching, with a heart so true
For a love that is mine, and a dream come true
And I'll hold on to hope, with every step I take
For the love that I seek, will soon be mine to make.
So I'll dance in the moonlight, with a smile so bright
For the love that I'll find, with each step tonight
And I'll hold on to hope, with a heart so true
For the love that I seek, will soon be mine and new.

28. STREET

The skies above, are a cloudy grey
A reflection of the pain, that won't go away
And the rain falls down, in a gentle shower
Washing away the sorrow, that's felt for hours.
The people pass by, with a hurried pace
Hiding their tears, and a sad embrace
And the street lamps flicker, in the lonely night
Shining a light, on the sadness in sight.
But still, there is beauty, in this place of pain
In the laughter that echoes, through the rain
And the love that shines, like a beacon bright
Guiding those lost, to a brighter light.
So I'll walk this street, with a heavy heart
And remember the love, that once had a start
And I'll hold on to hope, with a steadfast grace
For the sadness on this street, will someday fade away.

29. SEA

My love, my heart, my shining star,
You were lost, but now you are
Found in the depths of the Sea
Your beauty and grace, forever to be
Your smile, your laughter, a symphony
Echoes in my mind, forever will be
In the stillness of the sea you lay
But in my heart, you'll never decay
The waves may crash, the winds may roar
But nothing could diminish what we had before
I'll hold you close, within my soul
Where you'll forever shine, brighter than gold
So sleep well my love, in the Dead Sea's embrace
For I'll never forget your smiling face
In every sunrise, and every starlit night
You'll always be with me, my love, my light.

30. ONE

You are the one who makes my heart skip a beat
The thought of you, sends my soul to its feet
With every touch, my love for you grows strong
You are the only one, to whom I belong
Your smile, your laughter, your gentle embrace
Brings me a peace, I've never known to take place
In your arms, I find my safe haven from harm
You are my shelter, my home, my warm charm
Every moment with you, feels like a dream come true
With every kiss, I know, my love for you is true
You are the only one, whom I want by my side
Together we'll conquer, the highs and the lows of life
You are the one, who completes me and makes me whole
With you, my heart overflows with love, pure and bold
So, I promise to always cherish, hold and love you tight
Forever and always, my love, you are the only one in sight.